Nations of the
Western Great Lakes

Kathryn Smithyman & Bobbie Kalman

🌳 Crabtree Publishing Company

www.crabtreebooks.com

Nations of the Western Great Lakes

Created by Bobbie Kalman

Dedicated by Kathryn Smithyman
For Steve, whose integrity shines in everything he does

Editor-in-Chief
Bobbie Kalman

Editorial director
Niki Walker

Writing team
Kathryn Smithyman
Bobbie Kalman

Researcher
Molly Aloian

Editor
Amanda Bishop

Copy editor
Rebecca Sjonger

Art director
Robert MacGregor

Design
Margaret Amy Reiach

Production coordinator
Heather Fitzpatrick

Photo research
Laura Hysert
Jaimie Nathan

Consultants
Dr. Jon Parmenter, Assistant Professor, Department of History; Coordinator,
    Native American Studies Program, St. Lawrence University
Professor Leanne Simpson, Ph.D., Director, Indigenous Environmental Studies,
    Department of Native Studies, Trent University

Photographs and reproductions
William Armstrong/National Archives of Canada/C-10512: page 29
Lois Beardslee: pages 2, 30, 31
Beloit College, Logan Museum of Anthropology: page 11
Frances Anne Hopkins/National Archives of Canada/C-002775: pages 26-27
© Permission of Lazare & Parker: front and back covers, pages 12, 14, 15 (top),
    16, 20, 22, 23
© Permission of Lewis Parker: page 24
With permission of the Royal Ontario Museum © ROM: page 9 (bottom)
Smithsonian American Art Museum, Washington, DC/Art Resource, NY:
    pages 5, 9 (top)
Nativestock: page 15 (bottom)
© SuperStock: pages 8, 25, 28
The University of Michigan Exhibit Museum of Natural History: pages 1, 6, 7

Illustrations
Barbara Bedell: pages 10 (middle), 14, 20, 22
Katherine Kantor: pages 4, 7, 8, 10 (bottom right), 16, 17 (elm bark lodge), 18-19,
    21 (left), 23 (top), 24
Margaret Amy Reiach: border (pages 4-32), 6, 10 (top, bottom left), 12, 13, 15,
    17 (birchbark lodge and wickiup), 21 (right), 23 (bottom), back cover
    (hide background)
Bonna Rouse: background (pages 1-3), 4 (inset), 11, 17 (longhouse)

Crabtree Publishing Company

www.crabtreebooks.com   1-800-387-7650

PMB 16A	612 Welland Avenue	73 Lime Walk
350 Fifth Avenue	St. Catharines	Headington
Suite 3308	Ontario	Oxford
New York, NY	Canada	OX3 7AD
10118	L2M 5V6	United Kingdom

Cataloging-in-Publication Data
Smithyman , Kathryn
    Nations of the western Great Lakes/Kathryn Smithyman & Bobbie Kalman.
        p. cm. -- (Native nations of North America series)
Includes index.
This book introduces children to the traditional lifestyles of Native nations who lived in the western Great Lakes region, as well as the impact of colonization on Native peoples.
    ISBN 0-7787-0372-X (RLB) -- ISBN 0-7787-0464-5 (pbk.)
    1. Algonquian Indians--Juvenile literature. 2. Indians of North America--Great Lakes Region--Juvenile literature. [1. Algonquian Indians. 2. Indians of North America--Great Lakes Region.]
I. Smithyman, Kathryn II. Title.
    E99.A35 .K35 2003
    973.04973--dc21
                                                LC 2002012051

Contents

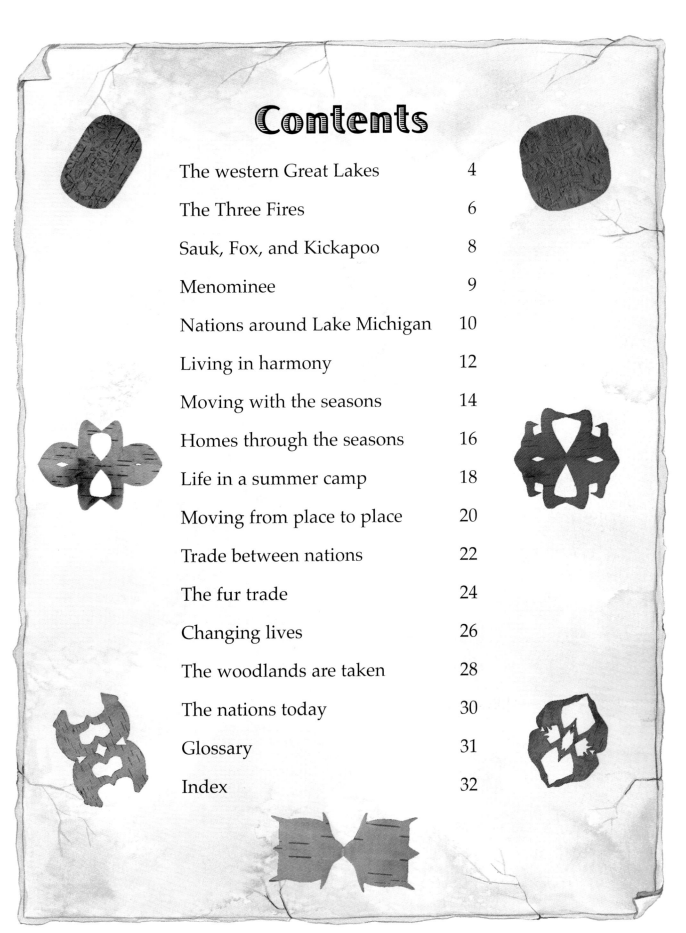

The western Great Lakes

The Great Lakes are five huge freshwater lakes in the northeastern part of North America. They are Lake Superior, Lake Michigan, Lake Huron, Lake Erie, and Lake Ontario. The land around Lake Superior, Lake Michigan, and to the west of Lake Huron is known as the western Great Lakes region.

Ancient origins

Indigenous, or Native, peoples have lived in this region for at least 12,000 years. The people lived in **camps** and villages in the forests and along the shores of the lakes.

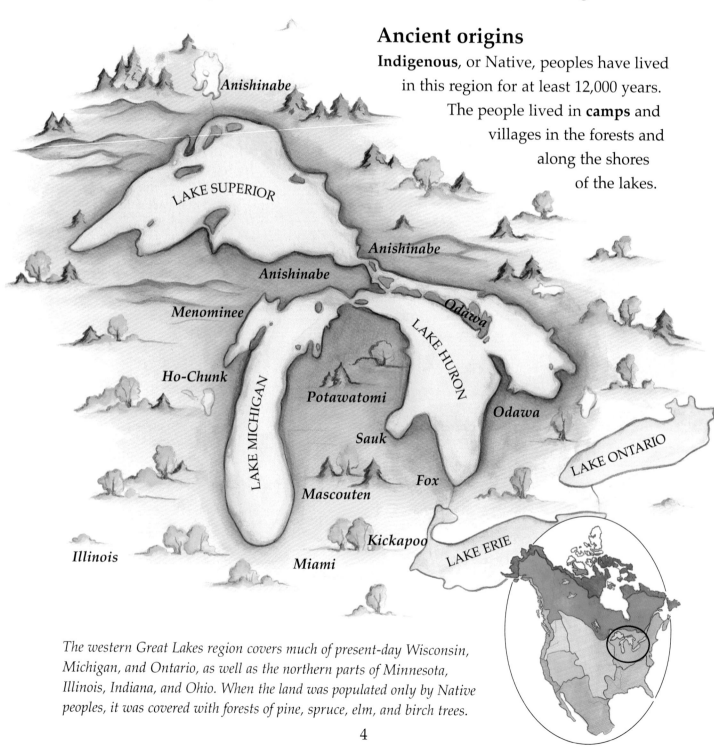

The western Great Lakes region covers much of present-day Wisconsin, Michigan, and Ontario, as well as the northern parts of Minnesota, Illinois, Indiana, and Ohio. When the land was populated only by Native peoples, it was covered with forests of pine, spruce, elm, and birch trees.

4

Many nations

The people of the western Great Lakes region lived similar lifestyles, but they were not all part of the same **nation**. The people of each nation wore different styles of clothing and practiced distinct customs and traditions. Some nations were made up of many people who were spread out over vast **territories**. Others had fewer people and smaller territories. The map on page 4 shows the location of each nation in the early 1600s. Members of a nation did not all live together in one place. Instead, they lived in large groups of **extended families** that included grandparents, parents, children, aunts, uncles, and cousins.

Different languages

The people of each nation spoke a different language. The Anishinabe language, for example, was different from the Odawa language. Both of these languages and many other western Great Lakes languages belonged to the same **language group**. The two main language groups in the area were **Algonquian** and **Siouan**. Almost all the western Great Lakes nations spoke a language that was part of the Algonquian language group.

Weather in the Great Lakes region changed from season to season. The people in this area moved throughout their territories and changed the foods they ate, the clothes they wore, and the homes in which they lived to suit the seasons.

The Three Fires

Three of the western Great Lakes nations—the Anishinabe, the Potawatomi, and the Odawa—were known as "The Three Fires." The people of these nations were so closely linked that they thought of their three nations as older, younger, and middle "brothers." People from these nations often married one another, traded goods, and made decisions together at **councils**.

Biting patterns into thin sheets of birch bark was a popular Anishinabe art.

Anishinabe

The Anishinabe are also known as Ojibwe, Ojibway, and Chippewa. The name "Anishinabe" means "the people" in their language. The Anishinabe nation was large, made up of many groups of extended families. The groups varied greatly in size, but most had between 300 and 400 people. The Anishinabe people lived across a huge area of land that spread north of Lake Huron and north and south of Lake Superior.

In the northern part of this territory, the people grew few crops. They mainly hunted, fished, and gathered the grains of grasses known as **wild rice**, which grew along the edges of lakes.

Potawatomi

The name "Potawatomi" means "people of the place of fire." The Potawatomi called themselves "Weshnabek," meaning "the people." Their territory—between Lake Huron and Lake Michigan—was perfect for growing tobacco, food crops, and herbs. The Potawatomi made medicines from the herbs. The soil in their area contained clay, which Potawatomi women used to make pottery.

Odawa

The name "Odawa" (Ottawa) means "to trade" or "at-home-anywhere people." The territory of the Odawa was near Lake Huron and on Manitoulin Island. In the early 1600s, there were about 8,000 Odawa living in this region.

Some Odawa lived on Manitoulin Island

LAKE SUPERIOR

LAKE MICHIGAN

LAKE HURON

Odawa

Like all Great Lakes nations, the Odawa hunted and gathered foods in the forests. They also fished with nets in Lake Huron and in the rivers that flowed into it. They made the nets by weaving strips of bark or plant stalks into rope, which they then wove into nets.

Each spring, the Odawa cleared an area for planting crops.

Sauk, Fox, and Kickapoo

*This Sauk **chief**, Wakechai (Crouching Eagle), wears a silver arm band. Some Sauk warriors wore necklaces and earrings made of silver.*

Kickapoo

The name "Kickapoo" means "he moves about, standing now here, now there." Although the people of the Kickapoo nation often moved from place to place, their territory was mainly west of Lake Erie, to the south of the Sauk and Fox nations. The Kickapoo carved many items, including bowls and tools, out of wood.

The Kickapoo carved wooden prayer sticks with symbols that reflected spiritual beliefs and important events.

Three nations—Sauk, Fox, and Kickapoo—lived similar lifestyles. The Sauk and Fox often formed **alliances** with each other to trade or to unite against enemies. Europeans often thought of these two nations as one nation.

Sauk

The name "Sauk" (Sac) means "people of the yellow earth." The Sauk people called themselves "Asakiwaki." They lived west of Lake Huron, although some historians believe that they may have lived near the southern tip of Lake Michigan at one time. Their territory had deposits of lead, which the Sauk mined and hammered into various objects, including tools and jewelry.

Fox

The Fox people called themselves "Mesquakie," meaning "people of the red earth." They lived southwest of Lake Huron. Besides growing beans and squash, Fox women gathered nuts, berries, and honey from the forests. Like the Sauk, the Fox mined and traded lead.

*This Fox warrior wears a headpiece, called a **roach**, made of deer and porcupine hair.*

Menominee

The name "Menominee" comes from an Anishinabe word meaning "wild rice people," but these people called themselves "Omenomenew." The large territory of the Menominee spread along the northwestern shore of Lake Michigan. The people harvested wild rice along the lake's marshy shoreline. This grain provided them with food year-round, so they did not move with the seasons as the other nations did. Menominee women made woven bags from the fibers of basswood trees. These bags were useful for carrying and storing wild rice and other foods.

A Menominee chief holds a sacred tobacco pipe.

The Menominee fished at night, using firelight to attract the fish, which they then speared. Traditionally they used torches, but in this painting the fires are contained in iron baskets. Beginning in the late 1600s, the Menominee traded with Europeans for iron and other metal goods.

Nations around Lake Michigan

In addition to the Menominee and Anishinabe, many other nations lived around Lake Michigan. These included the Mascouten, the Miami, the Illinois, and the Ho-Chunk.

Mascouten

In the Fox language, "Mascouten" means "little prairie people." The Mascouten originally lived on the southeastern shores of Lake Michigan, where their lifesyle was similar to that of the Fox and Kickapoo.

The Mascouten were forced out of their territory by the Haudenosaunee (Iroquois) between 1650 and 1700 and moved west. The Haudenosaunee wanted the Mascouten lands for hunting.

Miami

Historians believe the Miami, or "Omaumeg," as the Anishinabe called them, lived near the Kickapoo south and east of Lake Michigan. They were forced to move several times throughout their history, however, and were not always located in the western Great Lakes region. Their original name may have been "Twaatwaa," which sounds like the call of a crane. Most nations in the region relied on birch bark to make shelters and canoes, but the Miami did not have birch trees in their territory. In place of birch, they used elm bark, reeds, and butternut trees. The Miami traveled west to hunt **bison**, or buffalo.

Illinois

The Illinois called themselves "Inoca." "Illinois" (Illini) is a French pronunciation of this nation's word for "people." They lived south and west of the Great Lakes along the Mississippi and Illinois Rivers. Although they lived farther south than did most western Great Lakes nations, their culture was similar. Meat was the most important part of the Illinois diet. These people hunted buffalo, elk, bear, and turkey.

Ho-Chunk

The Ho-Chunk (Hochungra or Hotcangara) were the only people of the western Great Lakes region whose language was not part of the Algonquian group. It was part of the Siouan language family. In their language, "Ho-Chunk" means "people of the first voice" or "great fish nation." This nation is also known as "Winnebago," which comes from a Sauk and Fox word meaning "people of the dirty waters." The Ho-Chunk lived along the western shores of Lake Michigan. They moved less often than did the people of the other nations and built permanent homes. They planted crops, but their diet consisted mainly of fish. They fished using spears, bows and arrows, and **weirs**. Weirs are fences placed in water for trapping fish.

*In addition to fishing and growing crops, the Ho-Chunk also hunted. They dyed their clothing and baskets with plant dyes and decorated them with **quillwork**.*

Living in harmony

In addition to their extended families, most people also belonged to **clans**. The spirit of a familar and respected animal, such as a bear, deer, moose, or eagle, was considered the **ancestor** of each clan. Clan members honored the spirit of their clan animal, which was known as a **dodem** in the Anishinabe language. Some nations had many clans, whereas others had only a few. Although members of a clan were not always blood relatives, they were seen as "brothers" and "sisters." Marrying someone from the same clan was forbidden, so a husband and wife were always from different clans. The wife lived with her husband's clan but remained part of her own clan. Babies became part of their fathers' clans.

The value of humanity
In a Native community, every person was valued. Men and women often had different jobs, but their tasks were equally important to the survival of the community. Tasks such as hunting, fishing, and gathering plants for medicines were carried out by men, women, and children.

More than survival

In order to survive, Native people did many jobs such as hunting, preparing meals, and making clothing. There was much more to their lives than simply surviving, however. They valued beauty and decorated everyday items with quillwork, carvings, or paint. They considered gift-giving an honor, and many women made beautifully decorated clothing for their family members to show their pride and respect.

Group decisions

People in a village or camp usually gathered together to settle disagreements or to make decisions that affected the entire group. Both women and men were involved in the discussions. Each person had a chance to speak, but listening to others was just as important. When almost everyone agreed, a decision was made about what to do. Those who disagreed showed respect to the group by choosing not to oppose the decision.

Keeping the balance

Besides respecting one another, Native people also respected nature and everything that was part of it. Their survival depended on hunting animals, gathering plants, and fishing in the lakes, rivers, and streams. People appreciated the gifts of nature and offered thanks daily for the plants and animals they took. They never took more plants or animals than they needed, nor did they hunt or fish during the times when animals were **breeding**. They never wasted any part of an animal, either. They used the bones for tools, the skin for clothing, and the meat for food.

*People respected **elders** for their wisdom and experience. The elders told legends and stories that taught children the history of their people and respect for all things.*

Moving with the seasons

Family groups hunted and fished in specific areas at certain times of the year. These groups also had traditional areas in the forests where they gathered herbs, nuts, seeds, roots, and leaves. The men in this painting are cutting sheets of bark from the birch trees in their territory. People harvested bark in the spring. They used it to make canoes and homes.

The people of the western Great Lakes based their lives on the seasons. Almost all nations moved to find the foods that were available in different areas at various times of the year. The people of some nations moved several times a year, whereas others stayed mainly in one place. People who lived in the southern part of the region, such as the Ho-Chunk, were more likely to stay in one place most of the year because their territory had a long **growing season** for crops. The Ho-Chunk moved only twice each year, between their winter and summer camps. People who lived farther north, such as the Anishinabe, moved with every season.

Summer gatherings

Summer camps were often very large. Some Potawatomi summer villages were home to 1,500 people. Each summer, family groups returned to the same places to hunt, fish, gather food, and plant crops. Most groups did not change the location of their summer camps unless there were shortages of firewood or another nation forced them to relocate.

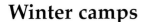

Winter camps

The snow and cold temperatures in winter made it hard to feed large groups, so people formed small winter camps made up only of immediate families. During the cold weather, people survived on stored foods and whatever animals they could catch. Men went on hunting trips as often as necessary, whereas the women and children stayed at the camp most of the time.

Other camps

In the spring and fall, most northern nations moved to camps where they gathered special foods to use during the rest of the year. For example, spring was maple sugaring season for the Anishinabe. In the fall, both the Anishinabe and Menominee harvested wild rice. These people moved to lakeshores to gather and dry the rice for use through the winter.

Buffalo hunts

Nations that lived west of Lake Michigan learned to hunt buffalo from neighboring **Plains nations**. The Fox, Kickapoo, Sauk, Menominee, Miami, Mascouten, and Ho-Chunk nations all made seasonal buffalo hunts. The Kickapoo hunted buffalo during the winter, whereas the Fox hunted it in the spring. Sauk men went on hunts in the fall, spring, and summer. All these nations relied on buffalo for meat and hides, which they used for food and clothing.

Homes through the seasons

People of all nations made homes using natural materials such as bark, wood, reeds, and hides. They built their homes to suit their lifestyles. Nations that moved very little lived for much of the year in villages with permanent houses and buildings. People who moved more often lived in communities made up of portable homes and storage buildings. Their dwellings, such as the reed-mat **wigwam** below, were designed to be taken apart and moved easily.

Wigwam lodges

Wigwams were portable, dome-shaped homes that were used as winter dwellings by most western Great Lakes nations. The word "wigwam" means "lodge" and comes from the Anishinabe word "wiigawaam." Some wigwams had oval bases, and others had circular bases. Each had a frame of flexible **saplings**, or young trees, which were bent at the tops and tied together. People then covered the frame with bark, reed mats, hides, or furs. Wigwams could be set up in less than a day. Families often took their wigwam coverings with them when they moved from one camp to the next but left the wigwam frames standing in each location.

16

Summer wigwams

The Anishinabe made summer as well as winter wigwams. Summer wigwams were large enough to house several families, whereas the winter wigwams housed just one. Most summer wigwams were covered in birch bark. Summer camps also included buildings that were used for meetings and storage.

birchbark lodge

Longhouses

Both the Odawa and Illinois built **longhouses**. A longhouse was a large, rectangular building with an arched roof. It had a framework of wooden poles that was covered with sheets of bark.

longhouse

Bark lodges

The Ho-Chunk made large wooden homes covered with bark or reed mats. Their villages also included other buildings, such as council houses, which were used for meetings and ceremonies. The buildings were arranged in two parallel rows, with an open area for games and ceremonies. The Menominee, Sauk, and Potawatomi also made bark lodges. The Sauk typically lived in areas where few birch trees grew, so they covered their lodges with the bark of elm trees. Potawatomi and Menominee lodges had peaked roofs.

elm-bark lodge

Wickiups

Kickapoo women built wickiups for their families. They lived in these dwellings from early spring until autumn. A wickiup had a wooden, dome-shaped frame covered in sticks and grasses. Whenever it was necessary, women added sticks to patch holes.

wickiup

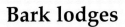

17

Life in a summer camp

Summer was a time for large gatherings. Although there was plenty of work to do, people took time to celebrate being reunited after their winter separation. Summer camps were usually made up of one nation, but some were shared by the people of several nations.

Food for the year

Many foods were available only in summer, so people worked together to gather and grow enough to last through winter. Men hunted and fished, while women gathered seeds, leaves, stalks, and fruits such as gooseberries, raspberries, and blueberries. They also looked for herbs, roots, and bark to use as medicines. Besides gathering food, women planted tobacco, beans, squash, and corn.

As fall approached, women gathered as many foods as possible and harvested their garden vegetables. They **preserved** some of the foods, or prepared them so they would not spoil. They dried herbs, fruits, vegetables, and some meat and fish. They smoked the rest of the meat and fish over a fire. Gathering and preserving food was as important as hunting. Many families relied on dried and smoked food during the winter months.

Moving from place to place

The Great Lakes are surrounded and connected by a network of rivers, streams, and smaller lakes. Native people used these waterways to travel throughout their territories to hunt, fish, trade, and fight wars. Traveling on water was often the fastest and easiest way to get from place to place.

Canoes were made by skilled men who offered thanks to the spirits of the trees before they cut them down or stripped their bark. Most canoes had wooden frames that were covered in layers of bark. The men harvested birch bark in the spring when it was full of sap. This moist bark could be formed into different shapes and did not shrink or stretch. Birch bark was the first choice for making watertight, lightweight canoes. If birch was not available, people used elm or spruce bark.

Different canoes

Most Great Lakes nations made several types of canoes. Each type was used for a specific purpose. People usually used small, lightweight canoes for traveling on small streams with calm waters. These canoes could be paddled by one or two people. The Great Lakes and many of the connecting rivers had rough waters, with high waves and rapids. Traveling on these waters required larger, heavier canoes with high ends and deep, V-shaped hulls to slice through the waves. Eight to ten people were needed to paddle and control these canoes, which were big enough to hold entire families or large loads of supplies.

*Some nations, including the Menominee and the Potawatomi, used dugout canoes for traveling on very rough waters. They used fire to **char** a tree trunk and then dug out the softened burnt wood.*

Moving on land

There were no roads, but there were paths through the forests and along the lakes and rivers. In most seasons, people walked from place to place when they were traveling on land. Walking in the winter, however, was slow and tiring when the snow was deep. To make traveling on the snow easier, people strapped **snowshoes** onto their feet.

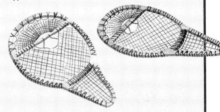

Snowshoes kept people's feet from sinking into the snow. Staying on the snow's surface kept feet dry and made walking much less difficult.

Sleds

Rivers and lakes often froze in winter, making it impossible to travel by canoe. To move people, belongings, and animals from place to place, many Native people used flat-bottomed sleds called **toboggans**. The sleds slid easily over the ice and snow. Most were big enough to carry a load of belongings as well as one or two people. Some people pulled their toboggans themselves, and others used dogs to pull them.

Trade between nations

Trade was an important part of life in the western Great Lakes region. When people gathered at camps in the summer, they often traded items they already had for items they needed or wanted. Foods that grew only in certain areas, such as wild rice, were especially valuable trade items. The Menominee, for example, traded wild rice with the Ho-Chunk in exchange for buffalo robes. Many nations traded with the Anishinabe in order to acquire the maple sugar they produced.

Certain territories contained resources that were not available in all regions. Menominee territory, for example, contained deposits of copper, which the people mined and hammered into many different items, such as bowls and jewelry. They offered copper and copper items to people of other nations, such as the Potawatomi. People also traded furs, beautifully carved objects, and woven baskets. The people of all nations made items for trade as well as for their own use.

"Place at the falls"
Water from Lake Superior flows into Lake Huron through a **strait** that forms a waterfall. The Anishinabe called this area "Bawating," meaning "place at the falls." The area of narrow waters was a valuable fishing spot for many nations. It was also a meeting place for people, such as the Sauk and Fox men shown left, to trade. Many French explorers and **fur traders** arrived there in the 1600s.

International trade

Native people not only traded with neighboring nations, but also with people from farther away. They traveled widely and often came into contact with other nations. While traveling, they saw tools, foods, and decorative items that their people did not have. The western Great Lakes nations traded extensively with the Haudenosaunee and Wendat (Huron) nations of the eastern Great Lakes. South of the Great Lakes area, several nations were eager to trade for products made of birch bark, since birch trees did not grow in their regions.

The fur trade

Contact between the people of the western Great Lakes and Europeans began after 1600. By this time, Europeans had been trading with the nations near the Atlantic Ocean for many years. The first Europeans who traveled to the western Great Lakes area were mainly French fur traders, who were eager to get mink, ermine, fox, marten, and otter furs. They valued beaver fur over all other types, however, because hats made of beaver fur were fashionable in Europe. European traders could sell the furs in Europe for a lot of money. The demand for fur drew thousands of French, British, and other Europeans to the Great Lakes area. Although some Europeans were trappers, many were traders who relied on Native people to trap large numbers of beaver and other animals.

In exchange, they offered the Native people European goods such as metal knives, cloth, and weapons.

Before long, European traders wanted more and more furs. They traveled farther into Native lands, and problems arose because most Europeans did not respect the traditional territories of the Native nations. They claimed lands and trade routes for themselves and forced Native peoples to move out of these areas.

Conflict between nations

When Europeans claimed land, it caused conflicts not only between them and Native peoples, but also among various Native nations. Some nations moved into the territories of other nations or invaded areas to trap more beavers for trade. Conflicts arose as a result. Later wars between nations were especially devastating, as more Native nations acquired guns through trade.

The European wars

Between 1689 and 1763, the French and British fought four wars for control of lands in the western Great Lakes region. Each country wanted to control the fur trade. Besides trading furs, the British also wanted to acquire Native territories so they could establish **colonies** that would be settled by their people.

Losing either way

Many Native groups in the western Great Lakes region were caught in the middle of these wars. Most sided with the French because the French were less interested in settling the land than the British were. Many Native people fought in the wars, believing that the Europeans would share the land and respect their place on it once the wars had ended.

British settlers

After the British defeated the French in 1763, however, they claimed all the lands for themselves. British **settlers** began arriving in the western Great Lakes region. They cut down huge areas of forest to build homes and establish farms. Clearing the land drove away many of the animals hunted by Native people and forced the people out of their traditional territories.

Changing lives

Contact with the Europeans completely changed the lives of Native peoples, including those in the western Great Lakes region. Along with metal and cloth goods, Europeans brought diseases, guns, and alcohol, which had a devastating effect on the Native way of life.

Diseases

Native people had never been exposed to diseases such as smallpox, typhus, measles, and influenza, which the Europeans brought with them to North America. Many became sick shortly after meeting the Europeans, and others were overcome with illness after handling European goods. The diseases spread quickly from one person to another in Native communities, and thousands died. In some areas, entire camps and villages were wiped out.

Relying on trade goods

Over time, Native people used more and more European goods in their daily lives. Guns replaced bows and arrows for hunting, and instead of sharp stones or shells, metal knives were used for cutting and scraping. Some people also relied on cloth rather than on animal hides for making their clothing. At first, they used cloth to make traditionally styled clothing, but eventually many Native people dressed in European-styled clothing.

Creating debt

At first, Native people traded just enough furs to get what they needed. European companies wanted more furs, however, so they offered Native people **credit**. With credit, people could get items they wanted immediately and would pay for them later. The trading companies then increased the prices of their goods but did not increase the prices they paid for furs. Many Native people went into debt

as a result of having credit. Hunters were forced to spend much of their time trapping in order to pay for the goods they had already received on credit.

Poisonous alcohol

European traders also introduced Native people to alcohol. They offered alcohol in exchange for furs and other trade items. Native people had never tasted alcohol, and even a little made them very sick.

Moving in permanently

Over the years, more Europeans arrived in the western Great Lakes region. They came not just to trade, but also to claim the land for themselves. They built homes and settlements in areas where Native peoples had formerly hunted, fished, and farmed.

*This painting shows British soldiers **portaging**, or carrying their canoes, around Kakabeka Falls. The site was originally a main Anishinabe portage route.*

The woodlands are taken

The idea that land could be owned as private property was not part of Native culture or beliefs. After 1763, however, the British claimed ownership of lands around the Great Lakes. After the American Revolution, some land was controlled by the British and the rest was controlled by the Americans. Neither group recognized the lands as "Native" lands. Native peoples were **displaced** from, or forced to leave, areas with British and American settlements. Some settlers simply forced them to move away from their villages with no regard for where they went. Usually, however, Native people were given agreements called **treaties** to sign. These treaties established that certain areas were for settlers and others were for Native groups. A few nations, such as the Miami, were forced to move out of the western Great Lakes region altogether. Others, such as the Anishinabe, negotiated treaties that enabled them to keep portions of their traditional lands. These lands are known as **reservations** in the United States and **reserves** in Canada.

Native people signed treaties to share the land with Europeans and Americans. This painting shows the signing of the Treaty of Greenville between the Americans and many western Great Lakes nations, including the Odawa, Miami, Potawatomi, and Kickapoo. The American government later broke this treaty. Europeans and Americans were often unwilling or unable to keep the promises they made.

European and American settlements took over the land and the waterways. Native people could no longer move from place to place with the seasons.

Forced to change

During the 1800s and into the 1900s, the governments of the United States and Canada wanted to "civilize" Native people by forcing them to give up their traditional ways of life. They took children from their families and placed them in boarding schools, where they were forced to speak English. Children were punished for speaking their Native languages. Boys learned European farming methods, and girls learned European household skills.

A difficult life

Both governments took control of lands and resources such as forests, fish, wildlife, water, and **minerals** such as copper and lead. They established laws that made it illegal to hunt and fish during certain seasons. These laws further disrupted the Native peoples' ways of life. The governments did not acknowledge that Native customs and traditions were respectful of lands, waters, and wildlife.

Few choices

Many Native people were forced to stay on reservations or reserve lands and establish farms. These lands often were not suitable for farming, however, and people could not support their families with their limited crops. Many reservations were far from towns and cities. There were few jobs besides farming, so people either had to leave the reservations in order to find jobs or face **unemployment**. Many Native people left to seek jobs elsewhere. Some felt pressure to give up their languages and cultures.

The nations today

Today, thousands of **descendants** of the western Great Lakes nations live throughout the United States and Canada. Many are working hard to preserve their heritage, language, traditions, and beliefs. Several nations have their own schools, which teach children Native languages and cultures. Some also have colleges, such as the College of the Menominee Nation. There are also several organizations founded by Native people to protect their rights and interests. Some protect natural resources; others ensure that Native people are treated equally under the law.

Many Native people, such as the artist shown below, value their ancestors and their cultures. They practice traditional ceremonies and art forms to show pride in their history.

Lois Beardslee is a contemporary artist from the Anishinabe nation. She makes bitten-birchbark artwork in the traditional way. An example of her art is shown on this page.

Glossary

Note: Boldfaced words that are defined in the book may not appear in the glossary.

Algonquian A group of related Native languages spoken by the majority of nations in the western Great Lakes region

alliance An association of two or more Native groups that is formed for the purpose of a common goal

ancestor A person, usually farther back in a family's history than grandparents, from whom someone is descended

breed To produce offspring

camp A group of people living in portable dwellings; the temporary village made up of these portable dwellings

char To burn the surface of something

chief The leader or head of a group

clan A group of people who are believed to share an animal's spirit as their ancestor

colony An area ruled by a faraway country

council A group of people called together to give advice, discuss problems, or make decisions

credit An agreement that allows a person to make a purchase and pay for it at a later date

descendant A person who comes from a particular ancestor or group of ancestors

elder An older, respected member of a family, group, or nation

fur trader A person who exchanges items for animal furs

growing season The length of time in a year when conditions are right for plants to grow

indigenous Describing people or things that are native to, or born in, a specific area

languge group Several languages that are similar to one another

nation A large group of people who share origins, customs, laws, leaders, and language

Plains nations Referring to the Native nations, such as the Sioux and Cheyenne, who lived on the Great Plains

quillwork The weaving together of quills, or the sharp spines of a porcupine, into decorative patterns

reservation (reserve) A specific area of land set aside by a government for Native people

settler A person who moves to a new place and makes it his or her home

Siouan A group of related Native languages spoken by nations from Lake Michigan to the Rocky Mountains

snowshoes A round or oval wooden frame with strips of leather woven across it, which is strapped to the foot and used to walk in snow

strait A narrow body of water joining two large bodies of water

territory An area of land and water on which a group of people traditionally lived, hunted, fished, and gathered food

tobaggan A long narrow sled made of thin wooden boards curled up at the front end and used to transport people or goods over snow

treaty A contract or agreement

unemployment The state of being without a job

wild rice The edible grain of a tall grass that grows in swampy areas bordering lakes or rivers

Index

This piece of contemporary art, titled "Manaboozhou Creating the Fishes," was painted by Lois Beardslee.

1 2 3 4 5 6 7 8 9 0 Printed in the U.S.A. 2 1 0 9 8 7 6 5 4 3